The Guitar Works of
AGUSTÍN BARRIOS MANGORÉ

**The First Definitive Collection of
Agustín Barrios Mangoré
Edited by Richard D. Stover**

Acknowledgements

The music in this book was collected during two trips to Central America, in particular El Salvador and Costa Rica. Most of the music was obtained from those people who knew Agustín Barrios Mangoré, and space does not permit a thorough listing of all the names of those who helped me in my work. However, I feel a special debt of gratitude to Lois, Dwight, Rebecca, and David Stover; Dr. John Marcum of Merrill College, UCSC; Roger Emanuels; Raymundo Barrera and family; Dr. Rafael Antonio Carballo; José Cándido Morales; Rubén Urquilla; René and Cortés Andrino; Carlos Payet; Juan de Dios Trejos and family; Julia Martinez de Rodriquez; Dr. Edgar Cabezas and family; and the Guitar Foundation of America.

Preface

This collection is the first comprehensive publication of the entire works of Agustín Barrios Mangoré, first guitarist/composer from the New World of truly universal importance. The significance of the works of Mangoré centers in their definition of a newer, more complex level of technique, influenced by but evolving independently from European models. The maturation of the guitarristic art as it is practiced in the countries of Iberoamérica has flowered in the genius of Barrios Mangoré.

This edition is not analytical nor comparative in its scope; it is designed for the performer, student and teacher. All accidentals are given as found in the original manuscripts. In very little of the music collected were there any fingerings given. Only after a thorough study of his works can one attempt to discern the most idiomatic solution consistent with Barrios' style and technique. For example, a salient feature of the way in which Mangoré used his left hand is its "stretched-out" aspect — in many pieces (such as *Estudio para Ambas Manos, Estudio del Ligado,* or *Choro da Saudade* to name a few) there are long, sustained reaches which can only be played in the way indicated to achieve the desired results.

In addition to written manuscripts, he also left a legacy of recordings, all made principally on the Argentine Odeon label, circa 1915-'30. When applicable, the recorded version of a piece has been taken as the preferred and final form, and many of the pieces are here presented for the first time in this corrected form corresponding exactly to what Mangoré played on his records.

Many pieces carried dates and dedications, and when justified all dedications have been translated from the original Spanish.

Contents

Biography Of Agustín Barrios Mangoré

Agustín Pío Barrios (b. May 5, 1885, d. August 7, 1944) was the greatest virtuoso guitarist/composer of the first half of the present century. Born in the small town of San Juan Bautista de las Misiones in Paraguay into a large family which esteemed both music and literature, he began to play the guitar at a very early age. He received his primary education in a Jesuit school where he utilized his guitar in the study of harmony. His first formal instructor, Gustavo Sosa Escalda, introduced young Agustín to the Sor and Aguado methods, as well as pieces by Tárrega, Viñas, Arcás, and Pargá. By the age of 13 he was recognized as a prodigy and given a scholarship to the Colegio Nacional in Asunción where, in addition to music, he distinguished himself in mathematics, journalism and literature. He also studied calligraphy and was a talented graphic artist.

Barrios, a great lover of culture, was quoted as having said, "One cannot become a guitarist if he has not bathed in the fountain of culture." In addition to Spanish he also spoke *Guaraní,* the native tongue of Paraguay. He read French, English and German and was keenly interested in philosophy, poetry and theosophy. He exercised daily and enjoyed working out on the high bar. He was warm, kind-hearted and spontaneous. Musically he was a tremendous improviser, and many stories are told of his completely spontaneous improvisations (many times in concert). His astounding creative facility enabled him to compose over 300 works for the guitar!

In his music we find truly inspired creativity combined with a total technical dominion of the guitar's harmonic capabilities. His knowledge of harmonic science enabled him to compose in several styles: baroque, classic, romantic and descriptive. He composed preludes, studies, suites, waltzes, mazurkas, tarantellas and romanzas, as well as many onomatopoetic works describing physical objects or historical/cultural themes. His most famous piece, *Diana Guaraní,* reenacted the War of the Triple Alliance which took place in Paraguay in 1864, complete with cannons, horses, drums, marching, and explosions! He also played a good deal of popular music, many of his finest compositions based on the song and dance forms found throughout Iberoamérica (cueca, choro, estilo, maxixe, milonga, pericón, tango, zamba and zapateado).

In 1932 he began to bill himself as "Nitsuga Mangoré — the Pagannini of the Guitar from the Jungles of Paraguay." Nitsuga (Agustín spelled backwards) and Mangoré (a legendary Guaraní chieftain who resisted the Spanish conquest) were used by Barrios for several years, after which he dropped this pseudonym to become simply Agustín Barrios Mangoré.

In addition to Paraguay, Barrios lived in Argentina, Uruguay, Brazil, Venezuela, Costa Rica and El Salvador. In these countries, as well as Chile, Mexico, Guatemala, Honduras, Panamá, Colombia, Cuba, Haití, Dominican Republic and Trinidad, he concertized continually from 1910 till his death. From 1934-'36 he was in Europe, playing in Belgium, Germany, Spain and England.

Perhaps over a hundred of his works still survive, either in manuscript or on the many 78 rpm records he made (over 30 records on 4 different labels). In addition to his own works, he played hundreds of other pieces, including all the standard works in the guitar repertoire up to that time (transcriptions of Bach, Haydn, Mozart, Beethoven, Chopin, Albéniz, Granados, as well as works of Sor, Aguado, Giuliani, Costé, Tárrega, Tórroba and Turina).

One can appreciate in Barrios Mangoré a logical expansion of techniques defined by masters such as Sor and Tárrega, carried to an even higher level of expressiveness and technical expertise. The legacy of his genius is a priceless one for all lovers of the guitar.

Richard Stover

Minueto en La
(Minuet in A)

AGUSTÍN BARRIOS MANGORÉ

Estudio No. 3
(Study No. 3)

AGUSTÍN BARRIOS MANGORÉ

Allegro

Estudio No. 6
(Study No. 6)

AGUSTÍN BARRIOS MANGORÉ

Don Pérez Freire
(Tango)

AGUSTÍN BARRIOS MANGORÉ

Junto a Tu Corazón-vals
(Close to Your Heart Waltz)

AGUSTÍN BARRIOS MANGORÉ

Preludio
(Prelude)

Composed February 2, 1939 in San José, Costa Rica for
Don José Francisco Salazar.

AGUSTÍN BARRIOS MANGORÉ

Andante appasionato

Minueto en Si Mayor
(Minuet in B Major)

AGUSTÍN BARRIOS MANGORÉ

Leyenda de España
(Spanish Legend)

AGUSTÍN BARRIOS MANGORÉ

Con ánimo

Escala y Preludio
(Scale and Prelude)

AGUSTÍN BARRIOS MANGORÉ

Minueto en Mi
(Minuet in E)

AGUSTÍN BARRIOS MANGORÉ

Dinora

San José, Costa Rica, July 12, 1939

AGUSTÍN BARRIOS MANGORÉ

"To the intelligent and dear child Dinora, beloved daughter of my unforgettable friend Don Walter Bolandi, in testimony of my sincere affection." - B. Mangoré.

EL 2603

Preludio
(Prelude)

AGUSTÍN BARRIOS MANGORÉ

Danza
(Dance)

AGUSTÍN BARRIOS MANGORÉ

Oración
(Prayer)

AGUSTÍN BARRIOS MANGORÉ

Estudio del Ligado
(Slur Study)

San Salvador, El Salvador July 29, 1941

AGUSTÍN BARRIOS MANGORÉ

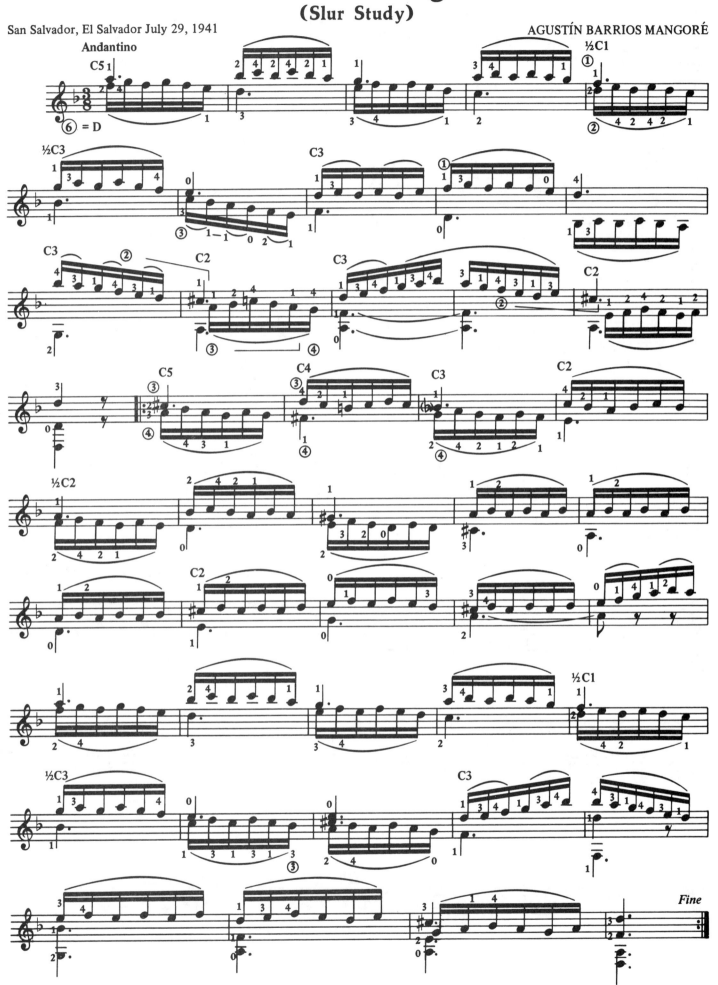

Estudio Vals
(Waltz Study)

AGUSTÍN BARRIOS MANGORÉ

Canción de la Hilandera
(Song of the Thread Spinner)

Mexico, March, 1933

Andantino

AGUSTÍN BARRIOS MANGORÉ

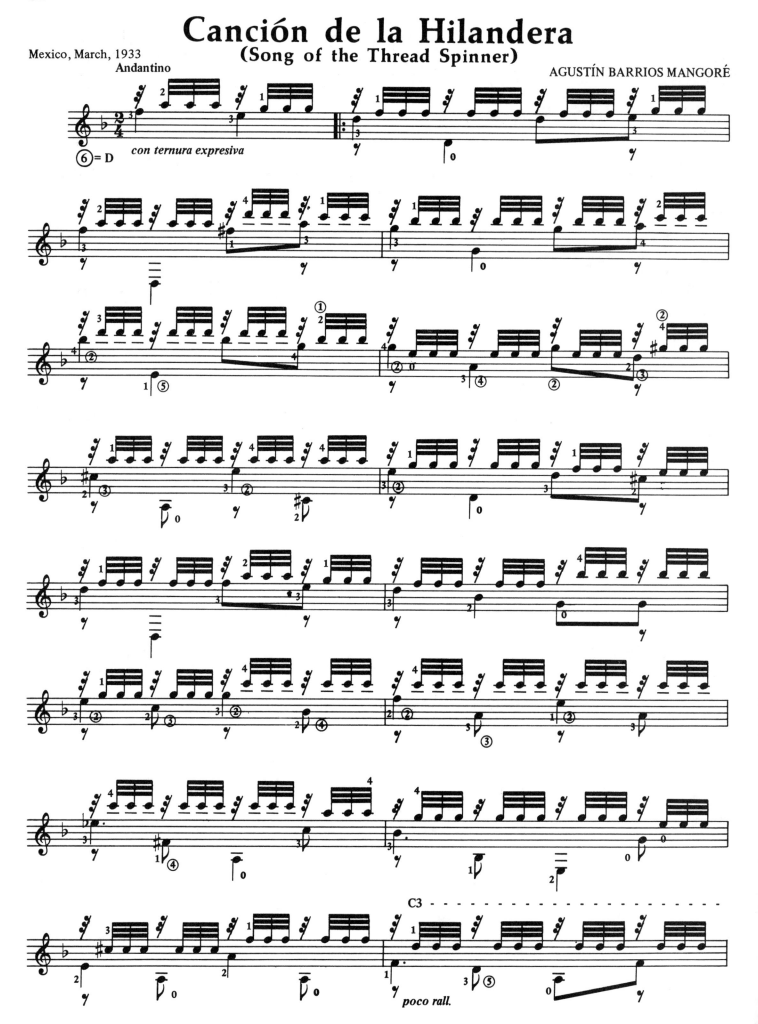

con ternura expresiva

⑥ = D

poco rall.

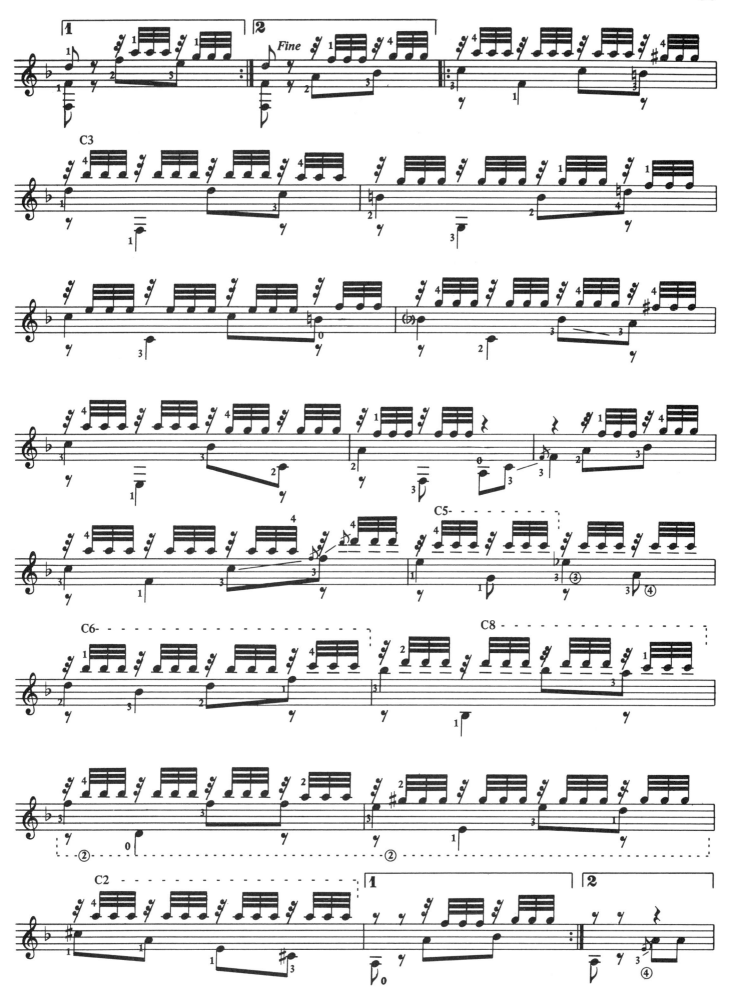

D. C. al Fine

Caazapá-Aire Popular Paraguayo
(Caazapá-Popular Paraguayan Song)

AGUSTÍN BARRIOS MANGORÉ

EL 2603

EL 2603

Romanza en Imitación al Violoncello
(Romance in Imitation of the Cello)

Moderato con alma

AGUSTÍN BARRIOS MANGORÉ

Canción de Cuna
(Cradle Song)

AGUSTÍN BARRIOS MANGORÉ